BARKS AND PURRS

CONTENTS

PREFACE 9
DRAMATIS PERSONAE 13
SENTIMENTALITIES 15
ON THE TRAIN 35
DINNER IS LATE 51
SHE IS ILL 72
THE FIRST FIRE 91
THE STORM 103
A CALLER 113

PREFACE

Madame:

There are moments when one seems to come to life. One looks about and distinguishes a creature whose foot-print closely resembles the ace of spades. The thing says: bow-wow. It is a dog. One looks again. The ace of spades is now an ace of clubs. The thing says: pfffffff—and it is a cat.

This is the history of the visible world and in particular, that of my god-children, Toby-Dog and Kiki-the-Demure. They are so natural—I use the word in the sense in which it is applicable to the savages of Oceania—that all their acts conspire to make of life, a very simple proposition. These are animals in the fullest sense of the word—animos—if I may employ the original orthography, capable of exclaiming with those of Faust:

>"The fool knows it not!
>He knows not the pot,
>He knows not the kettle."

* * * * *

And as such, Madame, you have placed them exactly where they should be: their earthly Paradise is the apartment of Monsieur Willy. In your salon, the probable palm and rubber-plant give the impression of luxuriant Edenic flora, relatively speaking, and illustrate the transmogrification which is to allow M. Gaston Deschamps—critic of a "Temps" plus-que-passé—to announce to the wilderness (where he speaks familiarly of Chateaubriand), and to the Collège de France, how well he can admire and understand a true poet.

* * * * *

For you are a true poet and I will declare it freely, not concerning myself more with the legends Parisians have the habit of weaving about every celebrity. They admire Gauguin and Verlaine, not so much for their originality, as for their eccentricities. And so it happens that certain persons, unacquainted with the nameless sentiment, the order and purity, the thousand interior virtues which guide you, persist in saying that you wear your hair short and that Willy is bald.

Must I then—living at Orthez—tell Tout-Paris *who you are, present you to all who know you—I who have never seen you?*

* * * * *

I will say then, that Madame Colette Willy never had short hair, that she does not wear masculine attire; that her cat does not accompany her when she goes to a concert, that her friend's dog does not drink from a tumbler. It is inexact to say that Mme. Colette Willy works in a squirrel's cage, or performs upon trapeze and flying rings, and can reach with her toe the nape of her neck. Madame Colette Willy has never ceased to be the plain woman *par excellence, who rises at dawn to give oats to the horse, maize to the chickens, cabbage to the rabbits, groundsel to the canaries, snails to the ducks and bran-water to the pigs. At eight o'clock, summer and winter, she prepares the café au lait for her maid—and herself. Scarcely a day passes that she does not meditate upon this admirable book*:

A LADY'S COUNTRY-HOUSE
BY
MME. MILLET ROBINET.

Orchard, kitchen-garden, stable, poultry-yard, bee-hive and hot-house, have no further mysteries for Madame Colette Willy. They say, she refused to divulge her secret for the destruction of mole-crickets to "a great statesman, who prayed her on his knees."

* * * * *

Madame Colette Willy is in no way different from the description I have just given of her. I am aware that certain folk, having met her in society, insist upon making her very complex. A little more, and they would have ascribed to her the tastes of the mustiest symbolists—and one knows how far from pleasing are those Muses' robes, how odious the yellow bandeaux above faces expressionless as eggs. Robes and bandeaux are to-day relegated to drawers in the Capitol at Toulouse, from which they will never be taken more, except when occasion calls for the howling of official alexandrines in honor of M. Gaston Deschamps, Jaurès, or Vercingétorix.

Madame Colette Willy rises to-day on the world of Letters as the poetess—at last!—who, with the tip of her slipper sends all the painted, laureled, cothurnèd, lyre-carrying Muses—that, from Monselet to Renan, have roused the aspirations of classes in Rhetoric—rolling, from the top to the bottom of Parnassus.

How charming she is thus—presenting her bull-dog and her cat with as much assurance as Diana would her hound, or a Bacchante her tiger.

See her apple-cheeks, her eyes like blue myosotis, her lips—poppy-petals, and her ivy-like grace! Tell me if this way of leaning against the green barrier of her garden-close, or of lying under the murmurous arbor of mid-Summer, is not worth the starched manner, that old magistrate de Vigny—with his neckcloth wound three times around, and rigid in his trousers' straps—imposed upon his goddesses? Madame Colette Willy is a live woman, a real woman, who has dared to be natural and who resembles a little village bride far more than a perverse woman of letters.

* * * * *

Read her book and you shall see how accurate are my assertions. It has pleased Madame Colette Willy to embody in a couple of delightful animals, the aroma of gardens, the freshness of the field, the heat of state-roads,—the passions of men . . . For through this girlish laughter ringing in the forest, I tell you, I hear the sobbing of a well-spring. One does not stoop to a poodle or tom-cat, without feeling the heart wrung with dumb anguish. One is sensible, in comparing ourselves to them, of all that separates and of all that unites us.

* * * * *

A dog's eyes hold the sorrow of having, since the earliest days of creation, licked the whip of his incorrigible persecutor in vain. For nothing has mollified man—not the prey brought him by a famishing spaniel, nor the humble guilelessness of the shepherd-dog, guarding the peace of the shadowy flocks under the stars.

A tragic fear shines in the cat's eyes. "What are you going to do to me now?" it seems to ask, lying on a rubbish-heap, a prey to mange and hunger—and feverishly it waits the new torture that will shatter its nervous system.

But have no fear . . . Madame Colette Willy is very kind. She quickly dispels the hereditary dread of Toby-Dog and Kiki-the-Demure. She meliorates the race, so that dogs and cats will learn in the end that it is less dull to frequent a poet than an unhappy Collège de France candidate—had this candidate proven more copiously still, that the author of "Mémoires d'Outre-Tombe" had topsyturvily described the jawbone of the Crocodile.

* * * * *

Toby-Dog and Kiki-the-Demure well know that their mistress is a lady who would do no harm—neither to a piece of sugar nor to a mouse; a lady who, for our delight, jumps a rope she has woven of flower-words which she never bruises, and with which she perfumes us; a lady who sings, with the voice of a clear French rivulet, that wistful tenderness which makes the hearts of animals beat so fast.

FRANCIS JAMMES.

* * * * *

DRAMATIS PERSONAE

KIKI-THE-DEMURE, A Maltese cat.
TOBY-DOG, A French bull-dog.
HE, }
SHE,} Master and Mistress (of minor importance).

SENTIMENTALITIES

    The sunny porch. TOBY-DOG *and* KIKI-THE-DEMURE *sprawl on the hot stone-flags, taking their after luncheon nap. The silence of Sunday prevails, yet* TOBY-DOG *is not asleep: the flies and a heavy luncheon torment him. Hind-quarters flattened out frog-fashion, he drags himself on his belly up to* KIKI-THE-DEMURE *whose striped body is perfectly quiet.*

TOBY-DOG

Are you asleep?

KIKI-THE-DEMURE, (*purrs feebly*)

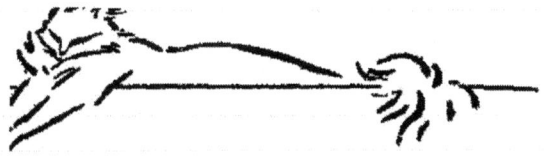

TOBY-DOG

Are you even alive? You're so flat! You look like the empty skin of a cat.

KIKI-THE-DEMURE, (*in faltering tones*)

L-e-t—m-e—a-l-o-n-e . . .

TOBY-DOG

Not sick, are you?

KIKI-THE-DEMURE

No . . . Let me alone. I'm asleep. I'm not even conscious of my body. What torment to live with you! I've eaten, it's two o'clock, let's sleep.

TOBY-DOG

I can't. Something's made a ball in my stomach. It means to go down I guess, but very slowly. And then,—these *flies*, these *flies*! The eyes start out of my head at the sight of one of them. I'm all jaws, bristling with terrible teeth (just hear them snap), yet the infernal things escape me. Oh! my ears! Oh! my poor, sensitive, brown belly! My feverish nose! There! . . . you see? . . . right on my nose! *What* shall I do? I squint all I can . . . two of them now? . . . No . . . only one . . . no, two! . . . I toss them up like bits of sugar and it's the empty air I snap . . . I'm worn out. I detest the sun, and the flies, and everything! . . .
(*He wails.*)

KIKI-THE-DEMURE, (*sitting up, his eyes pale from the light and sleepiness*)

Well, you've succeeded in waking me. That's all you wanted, isn't it? My dreams are gone! These flies that you're pursuing—I hardly felt their little teasing feet through my thick fur. The merest touch, like a caress, now and then thrilled along the silky sloping hairs which clothe me ... But then you never act with any discretion. Your vulgar gayety is a nuisance, and when sad you howl like a low comedian.

TOBY-DOG (*bitterly*)

If you woke up just to tell me *that*—

KIKI-THE-DEMURE, (*correcting*)

Of course you'll remember 'twas *you* woke me.

TOBY-DOG

I was so uncomfortable, I wanted someone to help me, to give me a word of encouragement ...

KIKI-THE-DEMURE

I don't know any digestive words.
(*Pause.*)
Fancy their giving *me* a bad character when ... Just examine your conscience a bit and compare us. Hunger and heat wear you out and drive you mad; cold makes your blood curdle ...

TOBY-DOG (*vexed*)

Mine is a sensitive nature.

KIKI-THE-DEMURE

A demoniacal nature, you mean!

TOBY-DOG

No, I don't mean that. You—you're a monstrous egoist.

KIKI-THE-DEMURE

Perhaps . . . You and the Two-Paws don't understand what you're pleased to call a cat's egoism . . . Our instinct of self-preservation, our dignity, our modest reserve, our attitude of weary renunciation (which comes of the hopelessness of ever being understood by them), they dub, in haphazard fashion, egoism. You're not a very discriminating dog, but at least you're free from prejudice. Will *you* understand me better? A cat is a guest in the house, not a plaything. Truly these are strange times we're living in! The Two-Paws, He and She, have *they* alone the right to be sad or joyful, to lick plates, to scold, or to go about the house indulging their capricious humors? I too have *my* whims, *my* sorrows, *my* irregular appetite, *my* hours of reverie when I wish to be alone . . .

TOBY-DOG (*attentive and conscientious*)

I'm listening, but I can hardly follow what you say. It's so complicated—a bit over my head, you know. But you astonish me! Are they in the habit of hindering you in your changeful moods? You mew, and they open the door. You lie on the paper—the sacred paper He's scratching on—He moves away, marvelous condescension!—and leaves you his soiled page. You meander up and down his scratching table, obviously in quest of mischief, your nose wrinkled up, your tail giving quick little jerks back and forth like a pendulum. She watches you laughing, while He announces "the promenade of devastation." How then, can you accuse Them—

KIKI-THE-DEMURE, (*insincere*)

I don't accuse Them. After all, psychological subtleties are not in your line.

TOBY-DOG

Don't speak so fast. I need time to understand. It seems to me—

KIKI-THE-DEMURE, (*shyly*)

Pray, don't hurry! Your digestion might suffer in consequence.

TOBY-DOG (*unconscious of the irony*)

You're right! I've some trouble in expressing myself to-day.—Well, here goes: it seems to me that of the two of us it's you they make the most of, and yet *you* do all the grumbling.

KIKI-THE-DEMURE

A dog's logic, that! The more one gives the more I demand.

TOBY-DOG

That's wrong. It's indiscreet.

KIKI-THE-DEMURE

Not at all. I have a right to everything.

TOBY-DOG

To everything? And I?

KIKI-THE-DEMURE

I don't imagine you lack anything, do you?

TOBY-DOG

Ah, I don't know. Sometimes in my very happiest moments, I feel like crying. My eyes grow dim, my heart seems to choke me. I would like to be sure, in such times of anguish, that everybody loves me; that there is nowhere in the world a sad dog behind a closed door, that no evil will ever come . . .

KIKI-THE-DEMURE, (*jeering*)

And *then* what dreadful thing happens?

TOBY-DOG

You know very well! Inevitably, at that moment She appears, carrying a bottle with horrible yellow stuff floating in it—Castor Oil! Wilful and unfeeling, she holds me between her strong knees, opens my jaws—

KIKI-THE-DEMURE

Close them tighter!

TOBY-DOG

But I'm afraid of hurting her—and my tongue, horrified, tastes the slimy mawkish stuff. I choke and spit, my poor face is convulsed and the end of this torture is long in coming . . . You've seen me afterwards dragging myself around, melancholy, my head hanging, listening to the unwholesome glouglou the oil makes in my stomach. . . .

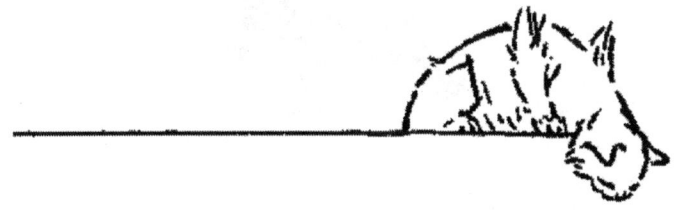

KIKI-THE-DEMURE

Once when I was little She tried to give *me* castor oil. I scratched and bit her so, she never tried again. Ha! She must have thought she held the devil between her knees. I squirmed, blew fire through my nostrils, multiplied my twenty claws by a hundred, my teeth by one thousand, and finally—disappeared as if by magic.

TOBY-DOG

I wouldn't dare do that. You see, I love her. I love her enough to forgive her even the torture of the bath.

KIKI-THE-DEMURE, (*interested*)

You do? Tell me how it feels. It makes me shiver all over, just to see her putting you in the water.

TOBY-DOG

Alas ... Listen then, and pity me. Sometimes, when She's come out of her tub with nothing on her but her skin, her soft hairless skin that I lick respectfully,—She spills out more warm water, throws in a brown brick which smells of tar, and calls, "Toby!" That's enough! The soul quits my body; my legs shake under me. Something shines on the water—the picture of a window all twisted out of shape—it dances about and blinds me. She seizes me, poor swooning thing that I am, and plunges me in ... Ye Gods! From that time on I'm lost ... My one hope is in her. My eyes fasten themselves on hers, while a close warmth sticks to me like another skin on top of mine ... The brick's all foamy now ... I smell tar ... my eyes and nostrils smart ... there are storms in my ears. She grows excited, breathes loud and fast, laughs, and scrubs me light-heartedly. At last She rescues me, fishing me out by the nape of my neck, I paw the air, begging for life; then comes the rough towel and the warm coverlet where, exhausted, I relish my convalescence ...

KIKI-THE-DEMURE, (*deeply impressed*)

Calm yourself.

TOBY-DOG

Jove! The telling it alone! ... But—you old sly-boots—didn't I see her one day armed with a sponge standing over *you*, holding *you* down on the toilet table?

KIKI-THE-DEMURE, (*quite embarrassed, lashing his tail*)

An old story! The long, fluffy hairs on my legs (which give them the outline of a Zouave's) had somehow gotten dirty. She insisted upon washing me. I persuaded her that I suffered atrociously under the sponge ...

TOBY-DOG

What a fibber you are! Did She believe you?

KIKI-THE-DEMURE

'Um ... at first. It was my own fault tho' when She didn't. Turned over on my back, I proffered the candid belly, the terrified and forgiving eyes of a lamb about to be sacrificed. I felt a slight coolness, nothing more. A fear that my sensibilities might be destroyed, took possession of me. My rhythmical wailings increased, then subsided, then went up again like the noise of the sea (you know the strength of my voice). I imitated the calf, the whipped child, the cat in the night, the wind under the door. Little by little I grew enraptured with my own song, so that long after She had finished soiling me with cold water I continued wailing, my eyes fixed on the ceiling. Then She laughed tactlessly and cried out, "You're as untruthful as a woman!"

TOBY-DOG (*with conviction*)

That *was* annoying.

KIKI-THE-DEMURE

I was angry with her the entire afternoon.

TOBY-DOG

Oh, as to sulking, you do your share! *I* never can. I forget injuries.

KIKI-THE-DEMURE, (*dryly*)

You lick the hand that chastens you. Oh it's well known!

TOBY-DOG (*gullible*)

I lick the hand that—yes, that's it exactly.—An awfully pretty expression.

KIKI-THE-DEMURE

Not mine... Dignity doesn't trouble *you* any! My word! I'm often ashamed for you. You love everybody. You take all sorts of rebuffs without even raising your back. You're as pleasant and as banal as a public garden.

TOBY-DOG

Don't you believe it, you ill-bred cat! You think you know everything and you don't understand simple politeness. Frankly now, would you have me snarl at His or Her friends' heels,—well-dressed people who know my name (lots of people *I* don't know know my name) and good-naturedly pull my ears?

KIKI-THE-DEMURE

I hate new faces.

TOBY-DOG

I don't love them either—whatever you say. I love—Her and Him.

KIKI-THE-DEMURE

And I, Him—and Her.

TOBY-DOG

Oh, I guessed *your* preference long ago. There's a sort of secret understanding between you two—

KIKI-THE-DEMURE, (*smiling mysteriously and abandoning himself to his reverie*)

An understanding, yes—secret and profound. He rarely speaks but makes a noise like a mouse, scratching his paper. It's for Him I've treasured up my little heart, my precious cat's heart, and He, without words, has given me his. This exchange makes me happy and reserved. Now and then with that pretty, wayward, ruling instinct which makes us cats rivals of women, I try my power over him. When we are alone, I point my ears forward devilishly as a sign that I'm about to spring upon his scratching paper. The tap, tap, tap of my paws straight through pens and letters and everything scattered about, is addressed to him as well as the insistent miauling when I beg for liberty. "Hymn to the Door-Knob," He laughingly calls it, or "The Plaint of the Sequestered Cat." The tender contemplation of my inspiring eyes is for him alone; they weigh on his bent head, until the look I'm calling searches and meets mine in a shock of souls, so foreseen and so sweet, that I must needs close my lids to hide the exquisite shyness I feel.

As for Her, she flutters about too much, often jostles me, holds my paws together and rocks me in the air, pets me in excited fashion, laughs aloud at me, imitates my voice too well—

TOBY-DOG (*moved with indignation*)

You're very hard to please! I certainly love Him; he's good and pretends not to see my faults, so that he won't have to scold, but She's the most beautiful thing in the world to me, the dearest and—the most difficult to understand. The sound of her step enchants me, her changeful eyes dispense happiness—and trouble. She's like Destiny itself, she never hesitates. Even torture from her hands—you know how She teases me?

KIKI-THE-DEMURE

Cruelly.

TOBY-DOG

No, not cruelly, but artfully. I never can tell what's coming next. This morning She bent down as if to speak to me, lifted one of my "tiny elephant's ears," as She calls them, and sent a sharp cry into it, which went to the very back of my brain.

KIKI-THE-DEMURE

Horrors!

TOBY-DOG

Was it right or wrong? I can't decide even now. It started waves of nervousness running madly through me. Then, She has a fancy for making me do tricks. Almost every day I must—"Do the Fish, Toby dear." She lifts me in her arms and squeezes me until I gasp. My poor dumb mouth opens as a carp's does when they're drowning it in air . . .

KIKI-THE-DEMURE

That's *just* like Her!

TOBY-DOG

Suddenly I find myself free—and still alive, miraculously saved by the power of her will. How beautiful life seems to me then! How fondly I lick the hand hanging at her side, the hem of her dress!

KIKI-THE-DEMURE, (*contemptuously*)

A pretty thing to do!

TOBY-DOG

All good and all evil come to me from Her. She is my worst torment and my one sure refuge. When I run to her, my heart sick with fear, how soft her arms are and how sweet her hair, falling in my face! I'm her "black-baby," her "Toby-Dog," her "little bit o' love." She sits on the ground to reassure me, making herself little like me—lies down altogether and I go wild with delight at the sight of her face under mine, thrown back in her fragrant hair. My feelings overflow, I can't resist such a chance for a jolly good game. I rummage and fumble about, excitedly poking my nose everywhere, till I find the crispy tip of a pink ear—Her ear. I nibble it just enough to tickle her—to make her cry out: "Stop, Toby! That's awful! Help! Help! This dog's devouring me!"

KIKI-THE-DEMURE

H'm! Simple, homely, wholesome joys! ... And then, off you go to make friends with the cook.

TOBY-DOG

And you,—with the cat at the farm.

KIKI-THE-DEMURE, (*coldly*)

Enough I pray, that concerns no one but myself ... and the little cat.

TOBY-DOG

A pretty conquest! It should make you blush—a seven-months-old kitten!

KIKI-THE-DEMURE, (*roused*)

For me she has all the charm of forbidden fruit and no one dare steal her from me. She is slim as a bean-pole ...

TOBY-DOG (*aside*)

You old rascal!

KIKI-THE-DEMURE

. . . and long; poised on long legs she walks with the uncertain step common to all young things. She hunts field-mice, shrew-mice—even partridge, and this hard work in the fields has toughened her young muscles and given a rather gloomy expression to her kitten-face.

TOBY-DOG

She's ugly.

KIKI-THE-DEMURE

No, not ugly, but odd-looking. Her muzzle with its very pink nostrils strongly resembles that of a goat, her large ears remind one of a peasant's coif, her eyes the color of old gold are set slant-wise, and their naturally keen expression is varied by an occasional piquant squint.

With what a will does she fly me confounding modesty with fear! I pass slowly by (one would think me quite uninterested), draped in my splendid coat. She's struck by its stripes. Oh, she'll come back, a little love-sick kitten, and putting aside all constraint she'll throw herself at my feet—like a supple white scarf—

TOBY-DOG

I've no objection, you know . . . I'm comparatively indifferent to all that concerns love. Here my time's so completely filled . . . physical exercise . . . my cares of watch-dog, I . . . hardly give a thought to the bagatelle.

KIKI-THE-DEMURE, (*aside*)

Bagatelle! . . . He indulges in the persiflage of a traveling salesman!

TOBY-DOG

I love—Her and Him devotedly, with a love that lifts me up to them. It suffices to occupy my time and heart.

The hour of our siesta is passing, my scornful friend. Do you know, I like you in spite of your scorn and you like me, too. Don't turn your head away, your peculiar modesty would hide what you call frailty and what I call love. Do you think me blind? How often, on coming back to the house with Her, have I seen your little triangular face at the window, light up and smile at my approach,—the time to open the door and you'd already put on your cat's mask—your pretty Japanesy mask, with its narrow eyes . . . Isn't it so?

KIKI-THE-DEMURE, (*resolved not to hear*)

The hour of the siesta is passing. The cone-shaped shadows of the pear trees grow long on the gravel path. We've talked away our sleepiness. You've forgotten the flies, your uneasy stomach, and the heat which dances in waves on the meadows. The beautiful, sultry day is dying. Already there's a breeze bringing perfume from the pines. Their trunks are melting into bright tears . . .

TOBY-DOG

Here She is! She's left her wicker chair, stretched her lovely arms and, judging from the movement of her dress, I think we're going to take a walk. See her behind the rosebushes? Now, with her nails she breaks a leaf from the lemon tree; she's crumpling it up and smelling it. Ah . . . I belong to Her, soul and body. With my eyes closed I can divine her presence.

KIKI-THE-DEMURE

Yes, I see Her. She is quiet and gentle for the time being. He'll leave his paper now to follow her. He'll come out calling, "Where are you?" and sit on the bench, tired out. For *him*, I shall rise politely, and go "do my nails" along the leg of his trousers. Silent, happy companions, we'll listen for the day's departing footsteps. The perfume of the lindens will become sickeningly sweet at the same hour that my seer's eyes grow big and black and read mysterious Signs in the air . . . Later on a calm fire will be lit down there, behind the pointed mountain—a circle of glistening rose-color in the gray-blue of the night—a sort of luminous cocoon from which will burst the dazzling edge of the moon. She will sail along, cleaving the clouds . . . Then, it will be time to go to rest. He'll carry me in on his shoulder and I'll sleep close to his feet, which are ever mindful of my repose . . . Dawn will find me shivering but rejuvenated, sitting face to the sun, in a silvery halo of incense, offered me by the dew. Thus, I am a perfect picture of the god I was in the old, old days.

* * * * *

ON THE TRAIN

KIKI-THE-DEMURE, TOBY-DOG, SHE *and* HE, *have taken their places in a first-class compartment. The train rolls along towards distant mountains, and the freedom of Summer-time.* TOBY, *on a leash, lifts an inquiring nose to the window.* HE *has strewn the carriage with newspapers.* KIKI-THE-DEMURE, *silent and invisible in a closed basket, is under his immediate protection.* SHE, *leaning back against the dusty cushions, dreams of the mountain she loves best and of the low house on it, weighted down with jasmine and virginia-creeper.*

TOBY-DOG

How fast this carriage goes! It can't be our regular coachman. I haven't seen the horses, but they smell very bad and make black smoke. Oh, Silent Dreamer, look at me and tell me—shall we arrive soon?

(*No response.* TOBY *gets fidgety and blows through his nostrils.*)

SHE

Hush! Toby, hush!

TOBY-DOG

I've hardly said a word . . . Shall we arrive soon?
(*He turns towards his master, who is reading, and puts a discreet paw on the edge of his knee.*)

HE

'Sh! . . .

TOBY-DOG (*resigned*)

Hard luck! No one wants to talk to me. I'm bored and what's more, I don't know this carriage well enough. I'm tired out. They woke me very early this morning. I amused myself by running all over the house. They had hidden the chairs under sheets, wrapped up the lamps, rolled up the rugs. Things were white and changed and awful. There was a horrid smell of camphor everywhere. My eyes filled with water, I sneezed under the chairs and slid on the bare floor in my haste to follow the maids' white aprons. They bustled about among trunks with such unwonted zeal, that I was sure something exceptional was going to happen.

At the last minute just as She came in, calling: "Toby's collar and the cat's basket! Quick! put the cat in his basket!"—just as she was saying that, my chum disappeared. It was indescribable! He, terrible to see, swore by all the gods, and struck the floor with his cane, furious because they had allowed his Kiki to get away. She called "Kiki!" at first supplicatingly, then in threatening tones, and the maids brought empty plates, meant to deceive, and yellow paper from the butcher's. I really thought my chum had left this world, when suddenly—there he was perched on top of the book-case, looking down on us with an expression of contempt in his green eyes. She put up her arms: "Kiki *will* you come down immediately! You are going to make us lose the train!" But he didn't come down and it made me dizzy—though I was on the ground—to see him way up there walking and turning about and miauling shrilly to tell us how impossible he found it to obey. He was about frantic and kept saying: "Heavens, he's going to fall." But She smiled skeptically, went out of the room and came back armed with the whip. The whip said, "crack!" twice only; then a miracle happened I think, 'cause the cat leaped to the floor, softer and more bouncey than our plaything, the ball of wool. *I* would have broken to pieces falling like that! ... He has been in this basket ever since ... (TOBY *goes to the basket.*) Ah! here's a little peek-hole ... I see his whiskers ... they're like white needles. Whew! What eyes! (*He jumps back.*) I'm rather afraid. One can't really shut a cat up; he always manages to get out somehow.... He must suffer, poor fellow! Perhaps if I speak kindly to him... (*he calls very politely*) Cat!

KIKI-THE-DEMURE, (*spitting furiously*)

Khhh!...

TOBY-DOG (*jumping back*)

Oh, you said a bad word! You look awful! Have you a pain anywhere?

KIKI-THE-DEMURE

Go away! I'm a martyr... Go away I tell you, or I'll blow fire at you!

TOBY-DOG (*ingenuous*)

But why?

KIKI-THE-DEMURE

Why!—Because you're free, because I'm in this basket, because the basket's in a foul carriage which is shaking me to pieces, and because the serenity of those two exasperates me.

TOBY-DOG

Would you like me to look out and tell you what one sees from the carriage window?

KIKI-THE-DEMURE

Everything is equally odious to me.

TOBY-DOG (*having looked out, comes back*)

I haven't seen anything . . .

KIKI-THE-DEMURE, (*bitterly*)

Thanks just the same.

TOBY-DOG

I mean I haven't seen anything that's easy to describe. Some green things which pass right close to us—so close and so fast that they give one a slap in the eye. A flat field turning 'round and 'round and over there, a little pointed steeple—it's running as fast as the carriage. Another field all red with blossoming clover has just given me another slap in the eye—a red slap. The earth is sinking in—or else we're going up, I'm not sure which. I see way off, *far* away, some green lawns dotted with white daisies—perhaps they're cows.

KIKI-THE-DEMURE, (*with sarcasm*)

Or wafers, for sealing letters—or anything you like.

TOBY-DOG

Aren't you the least little bit amused?

KIKI-THE-DEMURE, (*with a sinister laugh*)

Ha! Ask of the damned ...

TOBY-DOG

Of whom?

KIKI-THE-DEMURE, (*more and more melodramatic, but without conviction*)

... of the damned in his vat of boiling oil, if anything amuses him! Mine is not physical torment. I suffer imprisonment, humiliation, darkness, neglect—
(*The train stops. A conductor on the platform cries "Aw-ll a-bor!! ... awl aborr!!"*)

TOBY-DOG (*bewildered*)

Someone's crying out! There's an accident!! Let's run!!!
(*He throws himself against the carriage door and scratches madly at it.*)

SHE, (*half asleep*)

Toby dear, you're a nuisance!

TOBY-DOG (*distracted*)

Oh, you inexplicable person! How can you sit there quietly? Don't you hear those cries? They're stopping now—the accident has gone away. Wish I'd known . . .

(*The train starts again.*)

HE, (*throwing down his paper*)

The poor beast is hungry.

SHE, (*now very wide awake*)

You think so? Well, I am too. But Toby is to eat very little.

HE, (*anxiously*)

And Kiki-the-Demure?

SHE, (*peremptorily*)

Kiki sulks, and he hid this morning, so he'll have even less than Toby.

HE

He isn't making a sound. Aren't you afraid he's sick?

SHE

No, he's simply vexed.

KIKI-THE-DEMURE, (*as soon as there's question of himself*)

Me-ow!

HE, (*tenderly and eagerly*)

Come my beautiful Kiki, my imprisoned one, come. You shall have cold roast-beef and some breast of chicken . . .
(*He opens the prison basket and* KIKI *puts forth his head, flattened on top like that of a serpent; then his long, striped body, cautiously, and so very slowly that one begins to think it's coming out by the yard.*)

TOBY-DOG (*pleasantly*)

Ah, there you are, cat! Well, now, proclaim your freedom!
(KIKI, *without replying, smoothes his ruffled fur.*)

TOBY-DOG

Proclaim your freedom I tell you! It's the custom. Whenever a door is opened one must run, jump, twist oneself into half circles and cry out.

KIKI-THE-DEMURE

One? Who's one, pray?

TOBY-DOG

We dogs.

KIKI-THE-DEMURE, (*seated and very dignified*)

Would you have me *bark*, too? . . . We have never followed the same rules of conduct, that I know of.

TOBY-DOG (*vexed*)

Oh very well, I don't insist. How do you like this carriage?

KIKI-THE-DEMURE, (*sniffing fastidiously*)

It's frightful.—However, the cushions are rather good for one's nails.
(*He suits the action to the word.*)

TOBY-DOG (*aside*)

Now if *I* did that . . .

KIKI-THE-DEMURE, (*continuing to scratch the upholstery*)

Hon! May this spongy, gray cloth soothe my rage! . . . Since morning, the whole universe has been in a state of monstrous revolt. He whom I love, and who venerates me, made not the least effort to defend me. I've submitted to humiliating contacts, been jolted to death, piercing whistles have shot through my head from ear to ear. Ho, ho, how good it is to relax the nerves and to imagine that, with gleeful claws, one tears the enemies' flesh in bloody shreds! Ho, ho! S-c-r-a-t-c-h, and lift the paws on high! Lift them high as possible! It's a supremely insolent gesture . . .

SHE

I say, Kiki, when are you going to stop that?

HE, (*Indulgent and admiring*)

Let him alone. He's doing his nails.

KIKI-THE-DEMURE

He has spoken for me. I forgive him. But since it's allowed, I don't care any more about tearing the cushions . . . When will I get out of this? Not that I'm afraid; they are both there, and the dog too, with their everyday faces . . . I've twinges in my stomach.

(*He yawns. The train stops. A conductor on the platform cries, "Aw-ll a-bor! Aw-ll a-b-o-r-r!!"*)

TOBY-DOG (*excited*)

Screaming again! Another accident?!—Let's run! . . .

KIKI-THE-DEMURE

Heavens, what a tiresome dog! What does it matter to him, if there *is* an accident?

I don't believe in it moreover. It's the cry of a man, and men cry out for the pleasure of hearing their own voices.

TOBY-DOG (*calm again*)

I'm hungry. Can't we hope to eat soon, my mistress? I don't know what time it is in this strange country, but it seems to me . . .

SHE

Come now, we'll all have our luncheon.
(*She takes the things out of the basket, crumples up some tissue paper and breaks a crisp brown roll.*)

TOBY-DOG (*chewing*)

What She gave me then must have been very good indeed to seem such a tiny bit. It melted in my mouth, there's not even the memory of it left . . .

KIKI-THE-DEMURE, (*chewing*)

Breast of chicken! Purr-rr ... Goodness me! I was purring without knowing it! That won't do. They'll think me resigned to this journey. I must eat slowly, grim, and undeceived, eat for the sole purpose of keeping myself alive ...

SHE, (*to the dog and cat*)

Allow me to have *my* luncheon now, if you please. *I* too, like cold chicken and the hearts of lettuce, dipped in salt ...

HE, (*anxiously*)

What *shall* we do to make this cat go into his basket again?

SHE

I don't know. We'll see presently ...

TOBY-DOG

Finished already? I could swallow three times that much. I say Cat, you're eating rather well for a martyr.

KIKI-THE-DEMURE, (*fibbing*)

Trouble digs a hole in one's interior. Move away please, I want to sleep now ... if I can. Perhaps a merciful dream will take me back to the house I've left, to the flowered cushion He gave me ... Home! sweet home! Rugs of bright colors for the delight of my eyes, a palm with nice shoots for me to eat, deep arm-chairs, under which I hide my woolen ball as a future surprise for myself—ah, and the cork hanging by a string to the door-latch! the tables covered with bibelots! I thread my way in and out among them and occasionally it amuses me to break some brittle thing. The dining-room is a temple! The vestibule, full of mystery; there unseen, I can watch those who come and go . . . Oh narrow back-stairway, where the step of the milkman rings out for me like a morning angelus—farewell! farewell! my destiny carries me on, and who knows if ever . . . But this is *too* sad! All the pretty things I've been saying have really begun to make me feel badly!!

(*He begins a minute and mournful toilet. The train stops. A conductor on the platform cries, "Aw-ll-a-borr-a-borr!!"*)

TOBY-DOG

There it is again! An acci—Oh bother, I've had enough of that!

HE, (*anxiously*)

We're going to change trains in ten minutes. How about the cat? He'll never allow us to shut him up . . .

SHE

We'll see . . . Suppose we put some meat in his basket?

HE

Or perhaps petting would . . .
(*They approach the redoubtable* KIKI *and both speak together.*)

HE

Kiki, my beautiful Kiki, come jump on my knee, or on my shoulder. You like that as a rule. You'll doze there and then I'll put you gently into the basket. After all, it's open-work and has a comfortable cushion to protect you from the rough wicker. Come, my dear . . .

SHE

Listen, Kiki. You must learn to act properly and to take life as it is. You can't stay there like that. We're going to change trains and a horrible guard will appear and say insulting things of you and your race. Besides you'd better obey, because if you don't, I—I'll give you a good whipping.

(*But before she can lift her hand against his sacred fur, Kiki gets up, stretches himself, arches his back, yawns,—to show the rosy lining of his mouth, and then walks to the open basket where he lies down with an admirable air of quiet insolence. He and She exchange eloquent glances.*)

* * * * *

DINNER IS LATE

A parlor, in the country, at the close of a long summer's day. KIKI-THE-DEMURE *and* TOBY-DOG *doze; ears twitching and eyelids obstinately shut. Now* KIKI'S *lids part in a narrow slit, and disclose eyes the color of purple grapes. He yawns, with the ferocious expression of a small dragon.*

>KIKI-THE-DEMURE, (*haughtily*)

You're snoring!

>TOBY-DOG (*who was not really asleep*)

I'm not; it's you.

>KIKI-THE-DEMURE

Impossible! I don't snore, I purr.

TOBY-DOG

Same thing.

KIKI-THE-DEMURE, (*not condescending to a discussion*)

Thank heaven, it isn't! (*A silence.*)
I'm hungry. One doesn't hear the noise of plates in the next room. Isn't it dinner time?

TOBY-DOG (*gets up, slowly stretches his forepaws and yawns, darting forth a heraldic tongue with curly end*)

I don't know . . . I'm hungry.

KIKI-THE-DEMURE

Where is She? How is it you're not at her heels?

TOBY-DOG (*embarrassed, nibbling his nails*)

She's in the garden I believe, picking up plums.

KIKI-THE-DEMURE

Those yellow balls that rain about one's ears? I know them. You've seen her then? I bet She scolded you ... What have you been doing now?

TOBY-DOG (*self-conscious, turning away his wrinkled, toad-like face*)

She told me to return to the house because—because I too, was eating plums.

KIKI-THE-DEMURE

She did well! You have depraved tastes—the tastes of men.

TOBY-DOG (*offended*)

Say—no one ever sees me eating bad fish! And never, *never* will I understand how you can go into such fits over a dead frog, or that herb.

KIKI-THE-DEMURE

Valerian.

TOBY-DOG

That's it, I guess ... An herb—is medicine, isn't it?

KIKI-THE-DEMURE

Medicine, indeed! Valerian ... but no *you*, can't understand ... I've seen Her laugh and go on, as I do over the valerian, after having emptied a glass of fetid wine that jumped dangerously too. As for the dead frog—

so dead that it seems a bit of dry russia leather in the form of a frog—it's a sachet, impregnated with rare musk, with which I wish to scent my fur.

TOBY-DOG

Oh, you talk very well—but She always scolds and says that you smell bad after it, and He says the same thing.

KIKI-THE-DEMURE

They're nothing but Two-Paws, both of them. You, poor thing, belittle yourself by seeking to imitate them. You stand on your hind legs, wear a coat when it rains, eat plums—for shame!—and those big green balls, the malicious trees let fall sometimes, when I'm passing underneath.

TOBY-DOG

Apples?

KIKI-THE-DEMURE

Very likely. She picks one up and throws it down the path, crying: "Apple, Toby, apple," and you rush after, in unseemly fashion, gasping for breath, looking like a fool, your tongue and your eyes sticking out . . .

TOBY-DOG (*scowling, head resting on his paws*)

One takes one's pleasures where one finds them.

KIKI-THE-DEMURE, (*yawning, shows his pointed teeth and his palate of pink velvet*)

I'm hungry. Dinner is surely late tonight. Suppose you look for Her?

TOBY-DOG

I daren't. She forbade it. She is down there in the hollow, with a big basket. The dew is falling and wetting her feet and the sun's going away. But you know how She is. She sits on the damp ground, looking ahead of her, as if She were asleep—or lies flat on her stomach, whistling and watching an ant in the grass . . . She tears up a handful of wild thyme and smells it, or calls the tomtits and the jays—who never come to her by any chance. She takes a heavy watering pot and—ugh! it gives me the shivers—pours thousands of icy, silvery threads over the roses or into the hollows of those little stone troughs, 'way back in the woods. I always look in to see the head of a brindle-bull who comes to meet me and to drink up the pictures of the leaves, but She pulls me back by the collar with: "Toby, Toby, *that* water is for the birds." . . . Then She takes out her knife and opens nuts, fifty, a *hundred* nuts, and forgets the time . . . There's no end to the things She does.

KIKI-THE-DEMURE, (*shyly*)

And what do you do all that time?

TOBY-DOG

I—well—I just wait for her.

KIKI-THE-DEMURE

I admire you!

TOBY-DOG

Once in a while, squatting down, She eagerly scratches the earth, toils and sweats over it; then I jump 'round her, delighted to see her at something so useful and so familiar. But her feeble scent deceives her. *I* never smell mole, or shrew-mouse-of-the-rosy-paws, in the holes *She* digs. And how explain her utter lack of purpose? Presently, falling back on her haunches, She brandishes a hairy-rooted herb and cries: "I have it, the jade!" I lie in the damp grass and tremble, or dig my nose (She calls it my snout) into the earth to get the complicated odors of it. . . . When there are three or four scents all blended, all mixed together, can you distinguish that of the mole from that of the hare which passed quickly, or the bird which rested there?

KIKI-THE-DEMURE

Certainly I can. My nose is highly educated. It's small, regular, wide between my eyes, delicate at the chamois-skin end of my nostrils; the lightest touch of a blade of grass, the shadow of smoke tickles and makes it sneeze. It doesn't bother about distinguishing the scent of moles from that of—hares, did you say? But it delights in the trace left by a cat in a hedge ... I've a charming nose. She calls it, "his pretty little nose of cotton velvet." Since my eyes opened on this world I've not known the day that someone has not uttered a truthful flattery on the subject of my nose. Now yours—is a rough-grained truffle. What makes you move it so ridiculously? At this very moment.

TOBY-DOG

I'm hungry and I don't hear the plates.

KIKI-THE-DEMURE

... your truffle of a nose works up and down and makes another wrinkle in your irregular mug.

TOBY-DOG

She always says, "his square muzzle, his wrinkled truffle," so tenderly and so lovingly!

KIKI-THE-DEMURE

... And you think of nothing but eating.

TOBY-DOG

It's *your* empty stomach that scolds and complains and wants to quarrel with me.

KIKI-THE-DEMURE

I've a charming stomach.

TOBY-DOG

But no, it's your nose that's charming. You just said so.

KIKI-THE-DEMURE

My stomach too. There's none more fastidious, more whimsical, stronger and at the same time more delicate. It digests the bones of sole, but meat that's the least bit tainted literally turns it.

TOBY-DOG

Literally's the word. You have *active* indigestion.

KIKI-THE-DEMURE

Yes, the whole house is affected by it. From the very first qualms I'm in terrible distress; the earth gives way under me, my eyes dilate, I hurriedly swallow quantities of salty saliva; involuntary, ventriloquial cries escape me, my sides bulge out—

TOBY-DOG (*disgusted*)

I say, if it's all the same to you, tell me the rest after dinner.

KIKI-THE-DEMURE

I'm hungry. Where can He be?

TOBY-DOG

He's there, in his study, scratching paper.

KIKI-THE-DEMURE

He's always doing that. It's a game. Two-Paws play at the same thing for hours and hours. I've often tried to scratch paper gently, as He does, but the pleasure doesn't last long. I prefer newspapers torn into shreds that rustle and fly... There is a little pot of dark-violet, muddy water on his table. I never sniff it without horror, since the day a rather foolish curiosity made me dip my paw into it. This very paw, so strong and aristocratic, (the tufts of useless hair you see between my toes proclaim the purity of my race) this very paw bore a bluish stain for eight days and the degrading odor of rusty steel clung to it a long time after...

TOBY-DOG

What's the little pot for?

KIKI-THE-DEMURE

He drinks from it doubtless.
(*Silence.*)

TOBY-DOG

She's not back yet! Heaven grant She isn't lost, as I was one day in the streets of Paris!

KIKI-THE-DEMURE

I'm hungry!

TOBY-DOG

I'm hungry! What are we going to eat this evening?

KIKI-THE-DEMURE

I saw a chicken. It made a silly noise and dropped red blood on the kitchen floor, soiling it far more than I ever did, or you either—yet no one whipped it. But Emily put it in the fire, to teach it a lesson. I licked up some of the blood . . .

TOBY-DOG (*yawns*)

Chicken . . . it makes my mouth water. She'll say: "Here Toby, bones!" and throw me the carcass.

KIKI-THE-DEMURE

How badly you speak! He says: "Little chicken bones, Kiki, little chicken bones!"

TOBY-DOG (*surprised*)

But no *really* it's, "Here, Toby, bones!" that She says.

KIKI-THE-DEMURE

He speaks better than She does.

TOBY-DOG (*incompetent*)

Ah? . . . Tell me, do birds taste anything like chicken?

KIKI-THE-DEMURE, (*whose eyes light up suddenly*)

No . . . they're far better, they're alive. Ha, the quivering bird, the warm feathers, the delicious little brain . . . you feel it all crackling between your teeth!

TOBY-DOG

Oh, you make me sick! It always worries me to see tiny animals like that flutter about . . . and birds are dear, good little things.

KIKI-THE-DEMURE, (*dryly*)

Don't you believe it, they're only good to eat. They're noisy, stupid creatures, infatuated with themselves, *made* to be eaten. . . . You know the two jays?

TOBY-DOG

Not very well.

KIKI-THE-DEMURE

They live in the little wood. When I walk by they laugh a sardonic "tiac, tiac," because I wear a bell at my neck. In vain do I hold my head very stiffly and put my paws down *very* gently, my bell tinkles and the two creatures scream from the top of the fir-tree. Just let me get hold of them, one of these days! . . .

(*He lays back his ears and raises the hair along his back.*)

TOBY-DOG (*pensive*)

Positively, Cat, there are times when I don't know you. We are talking quietly and suddenly you bristle like a bottle-brush; or we happen to be playing amicably together and I bark behind your back—bow, wow-wow!—just for fun; then,—one doesn't know why, perhaps because my nose has grazed the long hairs on your legs you're so proud of—you become all at once a savage beast, spitting fire, and charging at me like a strange dog. Don't you think that shows a bad character?

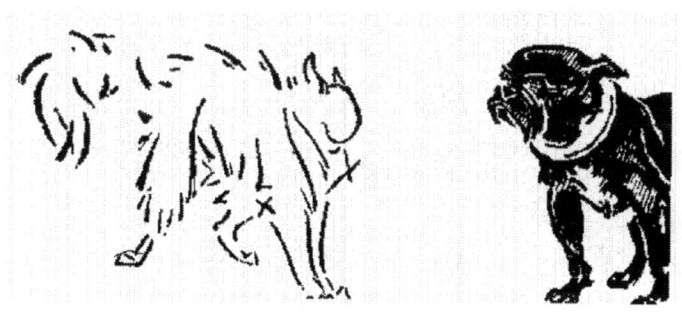

KIKI-THE-DEMURE, (*mysterious, eyes half-closed*)

Not at all. It's character, simply. A Cat's character. In such moments of irritability, I'm keenly alive to the humiliation of my present state, and that of my race.

I can remember a time when priests in long, linen tunics, bending low, spoke to us and humbly tried to comprehend our chanted utterance. Know, dog, that it is not *we* who have changed! It may be, there are days when I'm more myself, when everything offends me, and justly; a brusque gesture, a vulgar laugh, the banging of a door, your odor, your inconceivable impudence when you touch me, or encircle me, jumping and yelping . . .

TOBY-DOG (*patiently, to himself*)

He's having one of his attacks.

KIKI-THE-DEMURE, (*with a start*)

Did you hear?

TOBY-DOG

Yes, the kitchen door, and the door into the dining-room . . . and now the drawer where the spoons are kept. At last! At last! aaah! (*He yawns.*) I can't stand this any longer. *Where* is She? I don't hear the gravel creaking . . . night's coming on!

KIKI-THE-DEMURE, (*ironically*)

Go find her.

TOBY-DOG

And how about Him? He usually worries, and comes in asking, "Where is She?" But He's scratching still. He must have drunk up all the violet-colored water in the muddy little pot by this time. (TOBY *carefully stretches his legs.*) Ah! I feel lively . . . and empty. We're going to eat soon! Just smell the good kitchen-smells that come under the door! . . . Let's play!

KIKI-THE-DEMURE

No.

TOBY-DOG

Run, I'll chase, without touching you.

KIKI-THE-DEMURE

No.

TOBY-DOG

Why not?

KIKI-THE-DEMURE

I don't want to.

TOBY-DOG

Oh! but you're tiresome! Watch me jump and arch my neck like a little horse and try to catch my stubby tail. Now I turn 'round and 'round—and—heavens! the whole room spins!—It's—st—opping—now.

KIKI-THE-DEMURE

Insufferable creature!

TOBY-DOG

Insufferable yourself! Look out, I'm going to run at you as She does, when She's merry, crying "Ha, cat!"

(KIKI-THE-DEMURE, *without rising, puts up a paw bristling with claws and spotted underneath with rose color and black; it looks like a thorny flower.*)

If you dare! . . .

TOBY-DOG (*in a frenzy*)

I do dare! Bow-wow-wow! Ha, cat! ha, cat!
(KIKI-THE-DEMURE, *exasperated, gives a spring and hangs on the tablecloth, slowly dragging it down. A lamp and various things fall to the ground. Terrified silence. The two animals, crouching under an arm-chair, await punishment.*)

HE *appears at the study door, holding a pen, like a bit, between his teeth.*

Thunder and blitzen! What is it now? This cursed menagerie has overturned everything! Where's your Mistress? What a place this is to be sure! Dinner never on time! . . . (etc., etc., etc . . .)

(*The two guilty ones, who well know the harmlessness of such outbursts, laugh quietly to themselves and lying flat as bed-room slippers, look at one another through the fringes of the chair. The garden gate opens.*

SHE *comes in carrying a basket, full of fragrant plums; her hands are sticky from their sugariness, her hair tumbled.* SHE *stands horrified, before the disaster.*)

SHE

Oh! They've been fighting again, have they? (*Without conviction.*) Dear me, what nasty creatures! I'll give them away! I'll sell them!!—I'll *kill* them!!!

(*But the cat and dog, groveling in exaggerated humility, crawl up to her, and speak together.*)

KIKI-THE-DEMURE

Purr-rr-rr! . . . There you are! . . . It's very late . . . Toby attacked me; it's he who's broken everything. I believe he went mad from hunger . . .

You smell good, of grass and the twilight. You sat down on some wild thyme. Come! . . . Tell your Master to carry me on his shoulder—the meat will be overdone, I'm afraid. You'll carve the chicken very quickly, won't you, and you'll keep the browned skin for me? If you wish I'll stretch out my paw like a spoon, which knows how to take up the littlest morsels, and carry them to my mouth with that human gesture that makes you laugh so—you and He . . . Come!

TOBY-DOG

Hiii . . . hiii . . . there you are at last! I'm so unhappy when you're away. You banished me . . . you didn't love me . . . The lamp fell down all by itself . . . Come! I'm awfully hungry, but I'll gladly go without dinner, if you'll promise to take me with you always wherever you go . . . yes, even out in the twilight, though it makes me sad, I'll willingly follow you there . . . my nose close, close to the hem of your dress . . .

SHE, (*disarmed and quite indifferent to the cataclysm*)

Do look how pretty they are!

* * * * *

SHE IS ILL

A bed-room in the country-house; autumnal sunshine filters in through closed blinds. SHE *lies on a couch, apparently asleep, dressed in a white woolen gown.* KIKI-THE-DEMURE *makes his toilet on a narrow console-table.* TOBY-DOG, *on the carpet, in a sphinx-like attitude, watches* HER *and at the same time, is attentive to the words of his master, who is leaving the room on tip-toe.*

HE, (*in a very low voice to the two animals*)

Sh! Don't wake her. Be good. I'm going downstairs, to write. (*He closes the door noiselessly after him.*)

TOBY-DOG (*to* KIKI-THE-DEMURE)

What did He say?

KIKI-THE-DEMURE

I don't know. Something vague. Directions, like: stay there, good-by.

TOBY-DOG

He said, "'Sh!" *I'm* not making any noise.

KIKI-THE-DEMURE, (*ironically*)

They're astonishing! They say "no noise," and thereupon walk off with a step a deaf rat could hear two miles away.

TOBY-DOG

Some truth in that. (*He looks at the sleeping figure on the couch.*) Her face still looks very small. She's asleep. If you jump down from that table don't land with a big thump.

KIKI-THE-DEMURE, (*stiffly*)

Ah, you're teaching me to jump now, are you? Oh, worthy counselor! (*quoting*) Put a beggar in your barn and he'll make himself your heir.

TOBY-DOG

What's that?

KIKI-THE-DEMURE

Nothing. An Oriental proverb. If I wished, dog, to disturb the silence of this room I'd be clever enough to choose a rickety chair; its feet would pound out a regular tic-toc, tic-toc, tic-toc, in time with my tongue as I washed myself. It's a means I've invented to gain my liberty. Tic-toc, tic-toc, says the chair. She happens to be reading or writing, is easily irritated, and cries, "Be quiet, Kiki!" But I go on unconscious of any wrong-doing; tic-toc, tic-toc. She jumps up distracted and opens the door wide for me: slowly, like one exiled, I cross its threshold and once outside, laugh to find myself so superior to them all.

TOBY-DOG (*who hasn't been listening, yawns*)

What a sad week, eh? I don't know what it is to take a walk any more. I haven't taken any pleasure in eating either, since She fell from her horse.

KIKI-THE-DEMURE

Heavens, one can love people and care for one's stomach too.

TOBY-DOG (*with ardor*)

Not I! When She screamed and fell from her horse, I felt the heart crack inside me.

KIKI-THE-DEMURE

That affair couldn't have ended otherwise. One doesn't go climbing up on a horse! People don't do such things! I see nothing but extravagance around me. To begin with, a horse is a fearful monstrosity.

TOBY-DOG (*indignantly*)

Did one ever hear the like!

KIKI-THE-DEMURE, (*peremptorily*)

I happen to have had the opportunity of making a very close study of one...

TOBY-DOG (*aside*)

He makes me laugh!

KIKI-THE-DEMURE

... It was the farmer's horse that grazed in the meadow. My life, for a whole month, was embittered by that roving mountain. Lying under the hedge, I could see his heavy feet disfiguring the ground. I breathed his vulgar odor and heard his strident cry shaking the air. Once when he was eating the lower twigs of the hedge, I saw myself—the whole of me—reflected in one of his eyes! I fled . . . and from that day my hatred was so strong that I wildly hoped to annihilate the monster. I'll go up to him, thought I, I'll plant myself firmly in front of him, and the desire of his death will be so strong in my eyes, that perhaps, he'll die when he meets my look . . .

TOBY-DOG (*diverted*)

And then?

KIKI-THE-DEMURE, (*continuing*)

I carried out my plan. But the horse I had waited for in fear and trembling, just blew through his nostrils a long jet of foul-smelling vapor, and *I* fell back in atrocious convulsions.

TOBY-DOG (*Inwardly writhing with laughter*)

You don't exaggerate?

KIKI-THE-DEMURE, (*serious*)

Never! And She must needs go climbing on a horse's back, holding fast to four cords, one leg this side and the other that. . . . Strange aberration!

TOBY-DOG

We don't think alike, Cat. For me, the horse is, after man, the most beautiful thing in the world.

KIKI-THE-DEMURE, *(vexed)*

And where do I come in?

TOBY-DOG *(evasive and courteous)*

Oh, you're a *Cat*. But a horse, and with Her on his back! What a beautiful picture they make, high up in the blue air! To gaze on it, I have to throw my head 'way back on my thick neck. The horse lends her his speed. Now at last, She can race with me when I go off on a mad run. Sometimes I'm ahead, ears floating back and tongue hanging out like a little flag—the angular shadow of the horse on the road in front. If I follow her, a fragrant dust blows back at me. It smells of warm leather, moist beast, and a little of her own perfume too. The road runs under me, like a ribbon that someone is pulling. Oh, what joy it is to be so little and so swift, running along in the shadow of a great galloping horse! When we halt, I pant like a motor, between the legs of my friend, who snorts and in the kindliest way puts down his fettered mouth and sprinkles me . . .

KIKI-THE-DEMURE

I know, I know! The horse "with long mane ashake; hoofs, heavy with tumult; eyes, glimmering white." ... You are the last of the Romanticists.

TOBY-DOG

I'm not the last of the Romanticists. I'm a little bull-dog that came into the world one evening, almost under the feet of a chestnut mare. She didn't lie down all night long, she was so afraid of crushing my mother and her puppies. A little bull-dog like me is almost the child of a horse. I lay in the warm straw against her warm flanks, I drank out of the stable pails. I used to get up when I heard the sound of hoofs coming in and I took an interest in the washing of the carriages, until the day She came and picked me out—*me*, the best-looking, the most snub-nosed, the stockiest of the litter. (*Sighing.*) And there She lies, so dreadfully quiet! It makes me sad to see her with that little cloth still 'round her ankle. You remember when He picked her up in his arms? He held her—and She's a lot bigger than I am—just as if She were a little dog that he was going to drown . . .

KIKI-THE-DEMURE, (*bitterly*)

I remember. I was at the top of the stairs irritated by the noise, but curious. He came up and pushed me aside with his foot, as he would have done if a piece of furniture had happened to be in his way.

TOBY-DOG

Is that why you stayed away from this room—her room—for three whole days?

KIKI-THE-DEMURE, (*hesitating*)

Yes . . . and for another reason too.

TOBY-DOG

What reason?

KIKI-THE-DEMURE

Because of the fever.

TOBY-DOG (*carried away by his love*)

Her fever smells better than other peoples' good health!

KIKI-THE-DEMURE, (*shrugging his shoulders*)

And they talk of a dog's scent! Truly the convictions of Two-Paws are based upon childish fables. You know of course that fever—

TOBY-DOG (*in a low tone*)

Makes one afraid, yes.

KIKI-THE-DEMURE, (*in a low tone*)

Makes one afraid, gives one cold shivers down one's back, distaste for everything and uneasiness all over. One hesitates on the threshold of a room where there is fever, searching fearfully some hidden thing . . . She was in bed and burning hot. I looked at her a long time, ready to run, saying to myself: "Who can be with her there—behind the curtains—who is it stifles and torments her and makes her moan in her sleep?"

TOBY-DOG (*frightened retrospectively*)

There wasn't anyone, was there?

KIKI-THE-DEMURE

No one but He—and the fever. He, the most intelligent of Two-Paws, was leaning over her listening to her breathing, dimly aware of an invisible presence. I overcame my aversion and looked at her. I was melancholy and jealous. He must love her, thought I, to go so near and defend her, to kiss her, imbued as She is with the evil charm. Would He hold me to his heart, if I—

TOBY-DOG (*imperatively*)

'Sh!

KIKI-THE-DEMURE

What?

TOBY-DOG

She stirred.

KIKI-THE-DEMURE

No.

TOBY-DOG (*alert, looking at her*)

No . . . She didn't stir, but her thoughts did. I felt them. Continue.

KIKI-THE-DEMURE, (*who has recovered his equanimity*)

I don't know now what we were talking about.

TOBY-DOG

The fev—

KIKI-THE-DEMURE, (*quickly*)

Enough. Don't recall it. Fever is the beginning of the thing one never speaks of.

TOBY-DOG (*shivering*)

Yes, I know . . . I don't like an animal that can't move. You know what I mean . . .

KIKI-THE-DEMURE, (*laughing cruelly*)

Nor do I. I can only eat live birds, and as for the tiny mice, I prefer to swallow them, squeak and all . . .

TOBY-DOG

Why does it amuse you to horrify me? You've a certain vanity that I can't understand. It consists in exaggerating cruelties that are already real enough. You call me the last of the Romanticists, aren't you the first of the Sadics?

KIKI-THE-DEMURE

Oh dog, poisoned with literature! An eternal misunderstanding separates us. "I'm a little bull-dog," you replied just now, with that stupid sincerity which disarms me. Let me say to you in my turn, "I am a Cat." The name is sufficient dispensation. There is in me a hatred of pain and ugliness, an overmastering detestation of all that offends my sight, or my reason. When the concierge's cat dragged around his wounded paw, I threw myself upon him, fired by a righteous anger, and until he stopped his whining I—

TOBY-DOG (*supplicatingly*)

Don't tell me!

KIKI-THE-DEMURE, (*getting angry*)

Understand then, once and for all—if the pale recital of what I did upsets you—that I wished to abolish, to annihilate in that bleeding animal the suggestion of my own inevitable death . . .
(*They are quiet for a little while.*)

KIKI-THE-DEMURE, (*shuddering*)

This confinement does us no good. I would gladly go out into the soft sunshine and do "the bayadeer's dance," as He calls it, on the dry gravel among the leaves, which look like fried potatoes. Everything is yellow out-of-doors. My green eyes would reflect the golden sun and the flaming woods and so turn yellow too. . . . Now I'll think only of what is joyous and yellow, the beautiful, cold Autumn, the rosy dawn that leaves its colors in the foliage of the cherry-tree . . . Come, let's prove the strength of our legs and enjoy to the full the consciousness that youth has only just begun for us . . . Who knows, death may never come . . .
(*He jumps down from the console-table, without making the least noise.*)

TOBY-DOG (*stopping him*)

What are you going to do?

KIKI-THE-DEMURE

Scratch at the door, and strike up the "Hymn of the Sequestered Cat."

TOBY-DOG (*indicating the figure on the couch*)

And doubtless waken Her?

KIKI-THE-DEMURE, (*stubbornly*)

I'll sing in a very small voice.

TOBY-DOG

And you'll scratch with your tiniest claws, I suppose? Stay here quietly, He commanded it when He went away.

KIKI-THE-DEMURE, (*loftily*)

Does He command me? He beseeches me, and that's my only reason for obeying him.
(*He sits down again, apparently resigned, and yawns slowly.*)

TOBY-DOG (*yawning*)

You make me yawn.

KIKI-THE-DEMURE

On the contrary, it's you who bore me. (*Temptingly.*) You're thinking what a good thing freedom is, aren't you? . . . A hen has probably escaped from the chicken yard—what sport you're missing!

TOBY-DOG

You really think so?

KIKI-THE-DEMURE

I said: probably . . . Have you finished exploring that rabbit's hole?

TOBY-DOG (*disturbed*)

No . . . it's so very deep! I almost buried myself, hollowing it out yesterday. The earth that stuck to my muzzle had some of the animal's fur in it . . .

KIKI-THE-DEMURE, (*more and more satanic*)

I suppose you'll finish that to-morrow . . . or some other day.

TOBY-DOG (*sadly*)

Why not say next year, while you're about it?

KIKI-THE-DEMURE

What's the matter with you? Your shiny black lip hangs down an ell, and your froggy eyes glitter with tears. Are you crying?

TOBY-DOG (*sniffling*)

No . . .

KIKI-THE-DEMURE

Poor, sensitive heart, console yourself. You'll have your pleasures and your friends again. At this very moment the farmer's dog is crunching bones in the kitchen . . . to beguile the long wait for you.

TOBY-DOG (*overcome*)

Oh! oh! the farmer's dog!

KIKI-THE-DEMURE

She's not alone either; that great dane, the watch-dog, keeps her company.

TOBY-DOG (*rebellious*)

That's not true!

KIKI-THE-DEMURE

Go see.

TOBY-DOG (*after one bound toward the door*)

No, that would make noise.

KIKI-THE-DEMURE

You're right, it would.
(*A mournful silence follows.* TOBY *curls himself up like a turban and closes his eyes, because he feels like crying. His breath comes in little sobs.*)

KIKI-THE-DEMURE, (*absently, in a low, monotonous chant.*)

The dog . . . the little dog . . . the bones, the little dog . . . the rabbit . . . the great dane, the rabbit's hole . . . the little dog, the mutton bones . . . the rabbit's skin . . .

TOBY-DOG *at first endures the torture heroically; then his nerves betray him and lifting his head he howls—the long plaint of the abandoned dog.*

Wooo—oo—oooooo!

KIKI-THE-DEMURE, (*from the top of the console-table*)

Will you be quiet!

TOBY-DOG

Wooooooooo!!—oo—oooo—oo!

KIKI-THE-DEMURE, (*aside*)

That's it! That's it!

(SHE *wakes bewildered, still captive of her dreams, while the Cat listens patiently to the approaching step on the stairs, which means liberty for him and punishment for* TOBY-DOG.)

* * * * *

THE FIRST FIRE

Because it is raining and an October wind chases wet leaves through the air, She has lit the first fire of the season in the great chimney-place. KIKI-THE-DEMURE *and* TOBY-DOG, *in ecstasy, side by side on a corner of the warm hearth-stone, contemplate the flame with dazzled eyes and address their meditations to it.*

KIKI-THE-DEMURE, (*looking very like a cushion; no paws visible*)

Oh Fire, how splendid you are! You have come back more beautiful than my memory of you! You are hotter and nearer than the sun! The pupils of my eyes contract in your light, their lids half close, modestly hiding the joy I feel at seeing you again, and my inscrutable countenance shows but the semblance of a thought painted there in fawn color and black . . . Your crackling drowns the soft sound of my purr. Don't snap too much. Be merciful, O inconstant Fire! Don't sputter sparks on my fur. Allow me to adore you without fear . . .

TOBY-DOG (*half baked; eyes blood-shot; tongue pendant*)

Fire! Divine Fire! Here you are again! I am still very young, but I remember how awe-struck I was the first time Her hand woke you in this same chimney-place. The sight of a god as mysterious as you are was most impressive to a baby-dog just out of the maternal stable. Oh Fire, I've not quite gotten over my fear! Hiii! . . . You spit at me, something red that smarts . . . I'm afraid . . . Well, it's gone now.

How beautiful you are, Fire! Out from your ruddy center shoot tatters and shreds of gold, sudden spurts of blue, and smoke that twists upwards and draws queer shapes of beasts . . . Oh, but I'm hot! Gently, gently, sovereign Fire, see how my truffle of a nose is drying up and cracking, and my ears—are they not ablaze? I adjure thee with suppliant paw. I groan . . . ah . . . I can endure it no longer! . . . (*He turns away.*) Nothing is ever perfect. The east wind coming under the door nips my hind-legs. Well, it can't be helped! I'll freeze behind if I must, provided I can adore you face to face.

KIKI-THE-DEMURE

I am a Cat and therefore aware of all that you bring in your train, O Fire! I foresee winter; its coming both troubles and pleases me. I've already begun to thicken and embellish my fur-coat in its honor, the darker stripes are becoming black, my white tippet swells into a dazzling boa, and the fur on my belly surpasses in beauty anything that has ever been seen. What shall I say of my tail, broad as a club, with alternate rings of fawn-color and black, or of the sensitive, priceless aigrettes which spring from my ears? My ear-rings She calls them . . . What cat could resist me! Ah! the January nights, the serenades under a frosty moon, the dignified wait on the pinnacle of a roof, the encounter with a rival cat on the narrow top of a wall! . . . But I feel quite sure of my superior strength. I'll swish my tail, put back my ears, sniff tragically as one does before vomiting, and then lift up my voice—its modulations are infinite. I'll make it strong enough to waken all the sleeping Two-Paws. I'll vociferate, I'll whimper, pacing up and down the garden, my body distended, my legs bent outward, feigning madness to terrify the tom-cats!

TOBY-DOG

I know something of the changes and pleasures you foretell, Fire—for I'm a Dog. Already, it is raining in the garden. I suppose it's raining on the road too, and in the woods. The falling drops are not warm, as they were in the summer storms when my truffle, gray with dust, delighted in the damp smell that came from the west. The sky is troubled and the wind has grown strong enough to blow my ears out straight, like little flags. A sharp cry, such as I make when I beg, comes under the door. You'll be shining here every day, Fire; but I'll have to suffer for the right to worship you. For She'll continue to wander about, her head covered with the pointed hood which changes her so, that it frightens me. She'll put on wooden shoes too, and carelessly crush the puddles, the little heaps of mud, and the weeping mosses. I'll follow her, since I've promised to do so my life long (and also because I can't help it), I'll follow her, a forlorn and piteous object, shining wet, my belly covered with mud, until, through very excess of misery I'll forget, and ramble in the coppice, interested in every undulation of the grass, eager to revive the drowned scents in it . . . She'll become communicative when she sees me hurrying along and we'll talk: "Ha, Toby-Dog," she'll say, "ha! ha! a bird! There on the branch! Look! you booby! Now he's gone." She'll condole with me then, until I'm on the verge of tears. "Oh, my little black boy, my sympathetic cylinder, my batrachian love, how cold you are, how wet, how sad, how you suffer, oooo!" And before I'm able to judge of the sincerity of her pity, the tears will overflow, my throat contract, and we'll wail in unison . . .

Ah, but what delirious joy when the capricious wooden shoes turn again toward the house, hurrying to rejoin Him whom we've left scratching paper! They don't go half fast enough for me then! I jump 'round her, barking with delight to see the hill diminishing, our climb at an end, to smell the good stable smell and that of burning wood as we near the house. At last you shine forth, O Fire, O Sun, through the misty window pane! . . . I shall hardly have crossed the threshold when an overpowering sleepiness will dash me to the floor in front of you—you, who will reduce the mud on my belly to fine powder and change the water of the roads to smoky vapor.

KIKI-THE-DEMURE

A delightful glow penetrates my coat to the silky down, the impalpable colorless threads which protect my delicate skin. I feel myself swelling like a cloud. I must quite fill the room. My whiskers seem charged with electricity—a sign that I will sleep—but for the time being, the contemplation of your splendor and thoughts of the coming season keep me awake. It's raining. I shall not go out. I'll wait for the sun, or the dry wind, or better still, the frost. Ah, how the biting cold stimulates me! It lashes my lungs with handfuls of needles, and makes a *bonbon glacé* of my charming nose. The rollicking frost-sprite will blow his madness into me. She'll laugh and He too, leaving his scratching-paper, to see me vie with the leaves in bounds, leaps and wild whirlings, resembling a floating flurry of gray smoke rather than a Cat. To the top of a tree! Down again! Then seven turns after my tail! A perilous backward leap! A vertical jump, with aerial *danse du ventre*! Girations, sneezes, careering from the real to the dream, until in terror of myself, I come to a sudden stop . . . Everything turns before my eyes. I'm the center of a strange, spinning world . . . In my bewilderment (half-feigned) I'll make a little moo, like a cow, which will bring them both running to me,—She laughing, and He fearing something wrong. That will suffice to sober me, and with a bold front and noble mien, I'll regain this cushion near your altar, O Fire!

TOBY-DOG

This hearth-stone burns the horny pads of my feet. What shall I do? Move away? never! I'll toast to death rather than give up this redoubtable bliss. Heaven prevent Her coming, now! I've reason to fear the lash of the whip, and the magic words which mean exile: "Toby! that's stupid! I forbid you to roast yourself. You'll have sore eyes, and catch cold when you go out." That's what She says, while I regard her with a stupid look of utter devotion. But She's never duped by it. I hear noises upstairs, her step coming and going . . . I wonder is her vagabond fancy wearied at last?

This morning She whistled to me and in my haste to obey her, I rolled to the bottom of the stairs—being low and thick-set, with short legs, no nose, and almost no tail to balance me. Well, we set off. The last apples were rocking to-and-fro on swaying branches. My happy voice, a joyful shout from her now and then, the vain crowing of the cocks, the creaking of wagons on the road—all these sounds floated on a bluish, cottony, suffocating fog. She took me far, and many marvelous things happened on our way. We met terrible giant dogs. My proud bearing seemed to exasperate them, but I kept them back with a single look (besides, a closed iron gate rendered them powerless). I chased a rabbit into the thicket, though She cried loudly: "I forbid you to touch the little animal!" . . . My mother certainly gave me swift legs but they're short, and the white end of the little beast kept far ahead. A bush covered with red berries detained us a very long time. She sees no objection to eating strange things and I can truthfully say that I always taste everything She offers me, for I've great faith in her. But this morning—"Eat, Toby, nice berries. Eat! here are some rose-hips. Oh stupid! how can you not dote upon their delicious flavor? I assure you these are comfits of Mother Nature's making." In deference to her, I chewed a reddish ball; there were some rough hairs on it—put there doubtless by her teasing hand—and what was bound to happen, did happen . . . Khaha! My throat rejected the nasty "rosehip." . . .

But listen, Fire, what I saw after that, passes *my* understanding. It was in a wood where stiff leaves rustled. Had She carried you under her cloak, or do gods like you come at her bidding? I saw her hands pile up the wood, arrange flat stones in some mysterious fashion, and then, Fire, I saw the sparks flash and your joyous soul palpitate, grow big, soar naked and rose-colored, veil itself in smoke, snap noisily (for yours is a belligerent soul), agonize—and disappear... The world is full of incomprehensible things...

Last of all, on our way back, I discovered near the park gate—saw it before She did—one of those invincible beasts called hedge-hogs, the mere sight of which brings us dogs to bay. What madness to realize that an animal is hiding under that pin-cushion and laughing at me, and that I can do nothing, *nothing*! I implored her—She can do nearly everything—to pluck him for me. She began by turning him over with a little stick, as if he were a horse chestnut. "Astonishing," said She, "I can't find the top of him!" Then She took one of his spines between two fingers and carried him home that way—I dancing behind her—and put him in her work basket. After a while the horrid beast unrolled himself, stuck out a pig-like nose, opened two shiny rat's eyes and raised himself, holding fast by his little paws, which were exactly like a mole's. "How pretty he is," She cried, "a real little black pig." I stood near the table groaning with covetousness, but She didn't pluck him for me, not then, or ever, and perhaps the cook ate him... This cat's a dissembler. Maybe *he*... But away with care! I'm too excitable! I mustn't let myself think of these things. Life is beautiful, O Fire, since you illumine it... I'm going to sleep ... Watch over my unconscious body... I'm going... to sleep...

KIKI-THE-DEMURE

One would think me asleep because the narrow slit made by my parted eyelids, seems but the continuation of that velvety line, that bold crayon-stroke, a sort of Oriental make-up, uniting my eyelids and my ears. But I'm awake, keeping watch like a yogi, in a state of blissful ankylosis, conscious of all that's going on around me . . . My privileged eyes, Fire, do but behold you better when they're closed and I can count the various essences you mingle in a sparkling bouquet. Here in a flame of mauve-color and blue, glows the soul of a branch of arbor-vitae. Yesterday it waved a plume-like shadow on the garden walk . . . To-day, with its delicate twigs, it is but a writhing skeleton. She cut it with one stroke of the pruning scissors. Why? That it might breathe out its fervent blue and mauve-colored soul? For like me, She delights in your dance, Fire, and chastises you when you're quiet, with a stern pair of tongs. Sitting there with her head bent and her arms hanging along her sides, what does She read, I wonder, in that fiery rose which is the labyrinthian heart of you? . . . She knows a great deal certainly, but not as much as a Cat.

That thick tear on the log represents the anguish of a very old fir-tree, killed by the assiduous ivy. Just a short time ago I saw it struck down, lying on the grass, its foliage looking like a beautiful head of reddish hair.

I saw the axe that felled it, too. Its trunk weeps tears of resin, which trail along in drivel, then change to heavy, creeping flame. But the dry red locks break into lines of living fire, whistle and shoot innumerable jets of many colors underneath a broad gold wave that rolls voluptuously . . .

Ah, love . . . hunting . . . fighting . . . It's your light, Fire, that discovers these passions in the depths of my being. It's time the little winged creatures searching withered berries came near. I'll have them soon! I'll watch, motionless in the brushwood, wildly wishing that the earth itself might hide me, the muscles of my legs twitching with desire to make the spring, my chin trembling . . . Then, if I don't betray my hiding-place by an irrepressible quavering, frightening them away in one great commotion of wings and rustling branches! . . . But no, I'm master of myself. One bound at exactly the right moment and my feeble prey is panting under me. Oh, the ridiculous effort of a weak animal—its tiny ineffectual claws and pointed wings beating against my face! My jaws will open to the splitting point and my perfect nose wrinkle ferociously, for the joy of holding a living, terrified body. I'll know the intoxication of battle! I'll prance victoriously, shaking my head to torment the bird a little, for it faints away too soon between my teeth! Terrible to see I'll gallop towards the house, singing in a strangled voice, without loosening my grip, for He must stop his scratching to admire me, and She must give chase with distracted cries: "Wicked, savage cat! Drop that bird! drop that bird!! Oh, I beg of you! It hurts me so . . ." Ha! She never can have hunted . . .

I intend to astonish the world, Fire, during Winter's reign. The Cat that lives at the farm (She says the farmer's cat, while we say the Cat's farmer), the fellow that's so badly dressed, disfigured by the nose of a weasel, and seems to walk on stilts, his legs are so long—well, he sharpens his claws and regards me the while. Patience! He's strong, brutal, irresolute, and utterly lacks distinction. The slamming of a door terrifies him; he puts back his ears and flies, panic-stricken. Still, I've seen him kill a good-sized hen, without making any fuss about it. For a glance of the young cat's deceitful eyes, or right of precedence on the garden wall, for a word of double meaning, for nothing, but the fun of the thing—I'll take my chances with him! He'll learn that a mysterious silence can demoralize the enemy quite as effectively as murderous cries. The low garden wall seems to me a convenient place. Let him try his hoarse miauling in all possible keys! May his unsightly face, and more hideous body dislocate itself in a deceitful ataxia (for they're still at these old tricks)! I'll be proof against it all, and merely flash the green magnetism of my magnificent eyes upon him. His brows will fall under their persistent insult, a shudder will run along his spine, he'll do a few steps of our ancient war dance—forward, back, forward again. But I'll stand—motionless as the statue of a Cat. The green witchcraft of my gaze will strike terror and madness into my rival and soon I'll see him writhe, utter false cries, and, as a last resource, try to balance himself on the nape of his neck, like a forked pear tree, only to roll over shamefully into the potato field . . .

All that will come to pass, Fire, exactly as I've told it. To-day the future dawns in your new flame . . . I'm growing drowsy . . . My purr and your crackling are ceasing together . . . I see you still and already I catch glimpses of my dreams . . . The silky sound of the rain against the window is soft as a caress, and the water-pipe on the roof sobs low like a pigeon . . .

Don't go out during my nap, Fire. Remember, you're the guardian of my august repose—that delicate death, known as a Cat's sleep . . .

* * * * *

THE STORM

A suffocating summer's day in the country. The blinds of the house are half closed. Not a sound is heard from within; not a murmur from the parched garden, where even the sensitive leaves of the mimosa hang motionless.

KIKI-THE-DEMURE *and* TOBY-DOG *begin to feel uncomfortably conscious of the coming storm, which is yet but a slate-blue plinth thickly painted at the bottom of the dull blue sky-wall.*

TOBY-DOG (*restlessly lying first on one side, then on the other*)

No use! I can't be comfortable. What does this heat mean anyway? I must be sick. It began at breakfast; I didn't like the meat and sniffed disdainfully at my dog-biscuit. Something awful is going to happen. I haven't done anything wrong that I know of—my conscience is clear—

and yet, I'm suffering. There lies my chum, shivering and unable to sleep. I know by his quick breathing that he feels just as I do . . . I say, Cat?

KIKI-THE-DEMURE, (*irritably, in a low tone*)

Be quiet!

TOBY-DOG

What? You're listening to some noise?

KIKI-THE-DEMURE

No! *Heavens*, no! Don't mention noise. The mere sound of your voice makes the skin on my back go in waves like the sea.

TOBY-DOG (*frightened*)

Are you going to die?

KIKI-THE-DEMURE

I hope not. I've a sick headache. Can't you see the arteries throbbing under the almost hairless skin of my temples—the transparent, bluish skin that denotes a thoroughbred? It's atrocious! The veins on my forehead are like writhing vipers, and I don't know *what* gnome forges in my brain! Oh, be quiet! Or at least speak so low that the coursing of my agitated blood may drown the sound of your voice . . .

TOBY-DOG

But it's this very silence that oppresses me. I tremble and don't know why. I long for the familiar voice of the wind in the chimney, the slamming of doors, the whispering of the garden, the poplars' ceaseless rustle—it always sounds like a trickling spring—

KIKI-THE-DEMURE

The uproar will come, soon enough.

TOBY-DOG

Do you think so? I wish He'd scratch paper. It's an idle habit but an honored one. And see how listless She is, there in her wicker chair. Their silence frightens me more than anything. She seems asleep, but I can see her eyelashes move and the tips of her fingers, too. She's forgetting to play with the little balls of thread and doesn't sing, or whistle. She suffers just as we do . . . Do you think this can be the end of the world, Cat?

KIKI-THE-DEMURE

No. It's a storm. Heavens! how uncomfortable I am! If I could only get out of my skin, cast off this fleece which is smothering me, fling myself naked as a skinned mouse into a fresher atmosphere! Oh Dog, you cannot see the sparks that make every separate hair on my body crackle, but I feel them. Don't come near! A blue flame is going to shoot out of me . . .

TOBY-DOG, (*shuddering*)

Things are coming to an awful pass! (*He drags himself to the porch.*) What have they done to the out-of-doors? Look! the trees are all blue and the grass glistens like a sheet of water. What mournful sunlight! It shines white on the slate roofs, and the little houses over there on the hill look like brand new tombstones. A heavy odor, like bitter almond, creeps from the white bell-shaped blossoms of the daturas, and makes me feel sick and faint. Far away, some smoke, heavy as the perfume of the daturas, goes slowly up in a straight line and falls again—like a broken aigrette . . . But come and see for yourself!

(KIKI-THE-DEMURE *walks falteringly to the porch.*)

TOBY-DOG

My word, *you're* changed too, Cat! You look as if you were starving, your face is so drawn. Your fur is plastered down in some places and sticking up in others; gives you the expression of a weasel that had tumbled into oil.

KIKI-THE-DEMURE

Don't let that worry you! I'll regain my dignity—if ever another day dawns for us. To-day, I drag myself around unwashed, uncombed, like a woman out of love with love, and life . . .

TOBY-DOG

You say such distressing things. I think I'll whine and call for help. Perhaps I'd better go to Her, and look in her face for the comfort you refuse me. But She seems asleep now, in that wicker chair, and how can I read my fate in her eyes, when their lids are down. I'll lick her hand very respectfully and ever so lightly! That will wake her and oh, may her first caress drive away the evil charm!

(*He licks the hand hanging at the side of the chair.*)

SHE, (*with a scream*)

Heavens! how you frightened me! Was there ever such a ninny as this Dog? There! . . .

(SHE *administers a smart rap on the nose.* TOBY'S *nerves give way and he howls loud and long.*)

SHE

Quiet! Not a word I say! Out of my sight! I don't know what's the matter, but I hate you! And that Cat sitting there, looking at me, like a bump on a log! . . .

KIKI-THE-DEMURE, (*bristling*)

If She dares to touch me, I'll devour her!

(*Just at this dangerous crisis a low rumbling is heard, distant and then near. Impossible to tell whether it comes from the horizon, or arises in the house itself. All three lose interest in the quarrel.*

TOBY-DOG *and* KIKI-THE-DEMURE *slink away, as if responding to a signal, and seek shelter, one under the bookcase and the other under an armchair.* SHE *turns anxiously to the leaden-hued garden, and the great violet bank of cloud, which of a sudden is riven by a blinding streak of blue fire.*)

SHE, TOBY-DOG, KIKI-THE-DEMURE, (*all together*)

Oh!

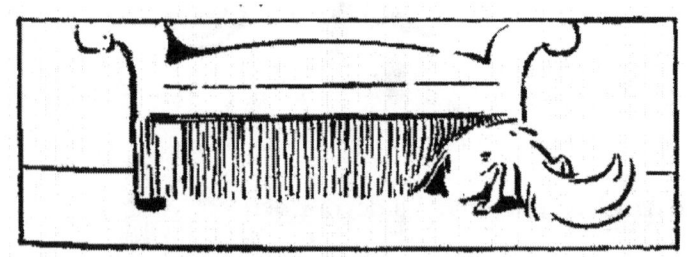

(*A sudden crash shakes the windows, and instantly a great rush of wind envelopes the house, with a noise as of flapping canvas:—all the garden prostrates itself.*)

SHE, (*in anguish*)

Heavens! the apples!

TOBY-DOG, (*invisible*)

I'll let them cut my ears into strips rather than leave this hiding-place!

KIKI-THE-DEMURE, (*invisible*)

I can't help hearing, and it's as if I saw everything that's going on. She hastens to close the windows. Someone is running on the stairs. Aïe! Another awful flame—and everything is falling in! Silence now . . . I wonder are they all dead? I'll look through the fringes of the chair, though it's risking my life to do so. Ah, hailstones making holes in the leaves! Here comes the rain, in silvery drops, wide apart, and so heavy that the gravel wrinkles up when they fall.

SHE, (*heart-broken*)

I can hear the peaches falling, and the green nuts too!
(*All three are silent. Rain; quivering streaks of lightning; hissing in the pine-trees. The wind howls. A lull.*)

TOBY-DOG

I'm not quite so afraid as I was. The sound of the rain relaxes my tired nerves. I seem to feel its streaming warmth on my ears and the back of my neck. Now the hubbub is further off! I can hear myself breathe. The light coming under this bookcase, is brighter than it was. What is She doing? I daren't go out yet. If only the Cat would move! (*He sticks out his head, like a wary turtle. A flash of lightning makes him draw it back again.*) Ha! It's beginning all over again. Rain by the bucketfuls against the window-panes. Something in the chimney is trying to imitate that far-away rumbling. Everything's falling to pieces ... and *She* gave me a rap on the nose!

KIKI-THE-DEMURE

Drop by drop, a little brownish river is filtering under the loose window-sash. It's stretching out and out on the floor, winding its way over to me. I'm so hot and thirsty, I'd like to lap up some of it. My joints ache and my ears are tired of standing up like weather-cocks at every crash. My jaws are still clenched with nervous fear. The seat of this chair is too low; it annoys me, rubbing against the fur on my back. However, it's some comfort to be able to *think* of such things—thanks to the peace that's descended on the house. The rain is falling quietly and the wind has gone down, but the memory of the din still hums in my ears. What can He be doing? The storm distresses him too. Why didn't He come forward to calm the raging elements? There She is, opening the porch door. Isn't it too soon? ... No, for the hens are cackling like old maids as they hop over the puddles. We're going to have fine weather. Oh, the adorable smell of wet leaves and earth refreshed! It's so new, so pure, I seem to breathe for the first time!

(*He creeps stealthily to the porch.*)

TOBY-DOG, (*suddenly*)

Um! How good! That smells like a walk! Things change so quickly one hasn't time to think. She's opened the door? Let's run! (*He dashes out.*) Well! well! the garden has got back its own color again! A warmish vapor moistens my rough-grained nose. I'm filled with the desire to jump and run. The grass is reeking, shining wet. Horned snails are feeling around in the pink gravel with the tips of their eyes, and speckled black and white slugs embroider the wall with a silver ribbon. Oh! what a beautiful green and gold beastie running out there in the wet! Shall I catch it? Shall I scratch its metallic shell, until it breaks with a little crackling sound? No. I'd rather stay near Her. She's leaning against the door, taking deep breaths and smiling quietly to herself. I'm *so* happy! Something inside me feels grateful to the whole world. The light is beautiful, and I'm quite sure that there'll never, never be another storm.

KIKI-THE-DEMURE

I shan't wait any longer; I'm going out. I'll find dry places between the puddles for my dainty paws to step on. An imperceptible thrill runs through the streaming garden, making the jewels hung all about, tremble and sparkle ... The slanting rays of the setting sun find their reflection in my eyes which are spangled with green and gold. Down near the horizon, where the sky is still unsettled, a glittering sword leaps up and puts to flight the dark, fuming cloud-horses, that have been galloping over our heads. Now the odor of the daturas rises and perfumes all the air, mingled with that of lemon leaves, bruised by the hail. The roses are crowned with midges. Oh sudden springtime! An involuntary smile stretches the corners of my mouth. I'm going to play at tickling my nostrils with the point of a sweet-smelling blade of grass, carefully stretching my neck to avoid the falling drops. But I want Him to follow and admire me. Will He not come out and enjoy himself with us?

(*A voice is heard humming the motif of the* Regensbogen: *sol, si, re, sol, la, si,—all flats. A door opens and closes again.* HE *appears under the dripping foliage of vines and jasmine, framing the veranda, and at the same moment, a rainbow is seen in the sky.*)

* * * * *

A CALLER

(*A winter's afternoon, in Paris. The studio; a fire crackles gently in the tower-shaped stove.* TOBY-DOG *and* KIKI-THE-DEMURE, *one on the floor, the other on his own particular cushion, proceed with the minute toilet which follows a long siesta. Peace reigns.*)

TOBY-DOG

My nails grow faster here than in the country.

KIKI-THE-DEMURE

It's the contrary, with mine.

TOBY-DOG

Really!

KIKI-THE-DEMURE, (*bitterly*)

Not to be wondered at! She clips them for the sake of the hangings ... Well! (*Magniloquently*), what can't be cured must be endured.

TOBY-DOG

What are you going to do to-day?

KIKI-THE-DEMURE

Why ... nothing.

TOBY-DOG, (*ironically*)

For a change I suppose.

KIKI-THE-DEMURE

Pardon, to *avoid* change. What is this rage for change that takes possession of you all? Change means destruction. Only that which remains stationary is eternal.

TOBY-DOG

I'm eternal then, these three hours past.

KIKI-THE-DEMURE

But you've been out with Her, haven't you? You came in like a whirlwind; bells rang, clothes were shaken out, you were sneezing and laughing and aureoled with icy air . . . The end of her nose felt so cold when She kissed me on the forehead. She always kisses me there, just over the dark stripes forming the classic M, which She assures me stands for miaou and for Minet, my name in French.

TOBY-DOG

Yes . . . we had a fine run on the banks of the fortifications, and then we went into a shop.

KIKI-THE-DEMURE

Is that amusing?

TOBY-DOG

Not often. There are a great many people crowded together. I'm immediately seized with the fear of losing Her, and I stick close to her heels, no matter what comes. Strange feet push and knock me about and step on my paws. I yelp but the skirts all around stifle my voice . . . When we're out of it, we both look as if we'd been shipwrecked . . .

KIKI-THE-DEMURE

May the gods preserve *me* from anything of the sort! Here, the moments have glided peacefully by. When She's not in this house, there's nothing to hinder me; I employ the time as my system of hygiene dictates. After my breakfast of rosy liver and milk, my kittenhood seems to come back to me; I'm filled with a foolish gayety. I go over to him. He's rumpling big, blackish papers and welcomes me with a quiet smile; we loll on the same divan, and revel in a few idle moments together. Sometimes, with imperious paw, I tear the paper He holds like a screen between us. It always seems to me the most desirable—the one that crackles best. He cries out, and I throw myself on my back and wriggle with joy in a sort of horizontal dance, He calls "the dance of the bayadeer." Then somehow, everything dwindles before my eyes, grows dim, and far away; I want to rise and go back to my cushion, but dreams already separate me from the world . . . Ah! blessed hour when you and She disappear, when the house is at rest and takes a long breath. Soon I'm in the depths of a dark, sweet sleep; my ears alone keep watch and turn like sensitive antennas towards vague sounds of doors and bells . . .

(*At this moment someone rings.* TOBY-DOG *and* KIKI-THE-DEMURE *start and change their positions. The Cat, sitting, encircles himself with his fluffy tail. The Dog, in a sphinx-like attitude, lifts his head boldly.*)

KIKI-THE-DEMURE

What's that?

TOBY-DOG

A tradesman?

KIKI-THE-DEMURE, (*shrugging his shoulders*)

That's not the kitchen bell. Perhaps it's caller.

TOBY-DOG, (*with a bound*)

What luck! They'll have tea and cakes! Come on!! Sugar, sugar! Little cakes! Little cakes!!

KIKI-THE-DEMURE, (*gloomily*)

To see ladies who shriek, and put gloved hands on my back—hands covered with dead skin? . . . ugh!
(*Feminine voices are heard—Hers among them—and the clear tinkling of a little bell; then the door opens and a very diminutive toy terrier enters, alone. She's black and tan, seems in love with herself, and comes forward with a mincing step.*)

THE LITTLE DOG, (*voice way up in her head*)

I'm the darling little dog, so pretty!

(TOBY *is struck dumb with admiration and astonishment.* KIKI, *indignant, has jumped on top of the piano and remains an unseen and hostile spectator.*)

THE LITTLE DOG, (*astonished at not hearing the chorus of admiration that everywhere greets her, is reciting—*)

I'm the darling little dog, so pretty! I weigh only one pound, eleven ounces, my collar is of gold, my ears of black satin, lined with shiny rubber, my nails are polished like the beaks of little birds. (*Catching sight of* TOBY-DOG.) Oh!—someone—(*silence*). He's rather good-looking.
(*They ogle and strut.*)

TOBY-DOG

How tiny she is!

THE LITTLE DOG

Sir—don't come near me.

TOBY-DOG

Why not?

THE LITTLE DOG

I don't know. My mistress knows. She's not here. She stayed in the other room.

TOBY-DOG

How old are you?

THE LITTLE DOG

Eleven months, (*reciting*) I'm eleven months old. At the dog show, my mother took first prize for beauty. I weigh only one pound eleven ounces and—

TOBY-DOG

You've said that already. What makes you so little?

KIKI-THE-DEMURE, (*from the piano*)

She's ugly, and has an evil odor. Her paws are deformed, she can't stand still an instant, and this dog takes pains to make himself fascinating!

THE LITTLE DOG, (*very coquettish and talkative*)

It's my lineage, of course. One can hold me in a muff. You've seen my new collar? It's gold . . .

TOBY-DOG

And what's that hanging from it?

THE LITTLE DOG

My mother's medal, Sir. I always wear it. I come from the *Palais de Glace*, where I made quite a hit. Imagine! I wanted to bite a gentleman who was speaking to my mistress. *How* they laughed!
(*She wriggles and chirps.*)

TOBY-DOG, (*aside*)

What an odd creature! Is she *really* a dog? (*Sniffs.*) Yes ... smells of rice powder, but it's a dog just the same. (*Aloud.*) Sit down a moment, it makes me quite dizzy to see you moving about so.

THE LITTLE DOG

Certainly. (*She lies down, like a miniature greyhound, crossing her fore-paws to show the slimness of her toes.*) You were here all alone?

TOBY-DOG, (*looking toward the piano*)

Yes, no other dog. Why?

THE LITTLE DOG

There's a strange odor.

TOBY-DOG

The Cat, doubtless.

THE LITTLE DOG

The Cat? What's a Cat? I've never seen one. Do they leave you in the room all alone?

TOBY-DOG

It happens so now and then.

THE LITTLE DOG

And you don't bark? *I* cry as soon as I'm left alone. I'm bored, afraid, feel sick, and chew up the cushions.

TOBY-DOG

And then you're whipped.

THE LITTLE DOG, (*insulted*)

I'm—what did you say? You're losing your senses, I imagine. (*Suddenly amiable again.*) That would be a pity. You have lovely eyes.

TOBY-DOG

Haven't I? They show well, don't they? They're large, and then they stick out. She says I have eyes like a lobster's, and sometimes She says "his beautiful seal's eyes, his frog-like eyes of gold."

THE LITTLE DOG

Who's She?

TOBY-DOG, (*simple*)

She.

THE LITTLE DOG

I don't understand all you say, but I find you so *very* sympathetic! What are you doing this evening?

TOBY-DOG

Why . . . I dine.

THE LITTLE DOG

Naturally! I wanted to know whether they receive here this evening, or do *you* go out?

TOBY-DOG

No, I've been out already.

THE LITTLE DOG

Driving?

TOBY-DOG

Walking—of course.

THE LITTLE DOG

Why, of course? I hardly stir except in a carriage. Show me the underside of your paws. Horrors! One would say 'twas the stone they sharpen knives on! Look at mine. Satin on top, velvet underneath.

TOBY-DOG

I'd like to see you in the country, on the cobble-stones.

THE LITTLE DOG

I've been there, Sir. I was in the country last summer and there weren't any cobble-stones.

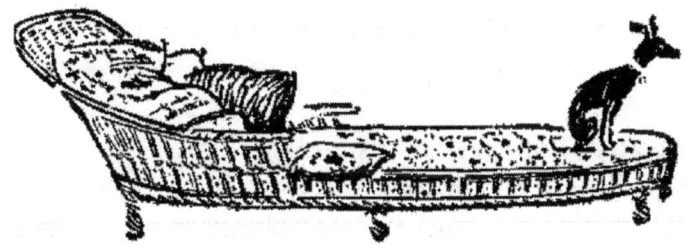

TOBY-DOG

Then it wasn't the country. You don't know what country means.

THE LITTLE DOG, (*vexed*)

Indeed I do, Sir! It's fine sand, and velvety lawns that are swept every morning; it's a reclining chair on the grass, great, fresh cushions of cretonne, foamy milk, naps in the shade, and charming little red apples to play with.

TOBY-DOG, (*shaking his head*)

No. It's the road covered with white powder that makes the eyelids smart and the paws burn, the tough, shriveled, sweet-smelling grass, where I scratch my nose and my gums; it's the fearful night—for I'm the only one to guard them, He and She. I lie in my basket, but the beating of my poor overdriven heart keeps me awake. I hear a dog crying to me from far off, that the Bad Man has passed on the road. Is he coming in my direction? Will I be obliged in another minute, my eyes bloodshot and tongue dry as chalk, to throw myself upon him and devour his shadowy face? . . .

THE LITTLE DOG, (*trembling and in ecstasy*)

Go on! Go on! Oh! how frightened I am! . . .

TOBY-DOG, (*modestly*)

Don't be afraid—it has never happened. All that is the country, yes, and the interminable hill, in the shadow of the carriage, when thirst, hunger, heat and fatigue, render the soul submissive and hopeless . . .

THE LITTLE DOG, (*quite worked up*)

And then?

TOBY-DOG

Oh, nothing. One arrives at the house, after all, and the pail of dark water, one drinks without taking breath, ("his tongue," She says, "his big tongue is parted in the center, like an iris-petal") while sore eyelids and dusty lashes are splashed with cooling drops . . . The country is all that and many things besides . . .

KIKI-THE-DEMURE, (*on the piano, musingly*)

All that, yes . . . and the habits of the year before that one finds again, molded to one's shape, like a cushion marked with the imprint of a long sleep . . . the long nights of freedom, when the lone owlet, with his sad little laugh, makes his way through the air as quietly as I do on the ground, and silvery gray rats cling to the vines, eating grapes and keeping their eyes on me at the same time. It's the sun-cure on the hot stone-wall, from which I arise wan and shrunken, baked through and through, but svelte enough to make the youngest tomcat envious. (*Coming back to the present with a murderous look at* THE LITTLE DOG.) Death to you, ill-smelling beast, for having evoked these by-gone joys! Aren't you going to disappear, that I may come down from this cold pedestal, where my paws are growing numb?

TOBY-DOG, (*enthusiastically to* THE LITTLE DOG)

But let us forget all that! With you there, I can think of nothing but you. I feel that I love you!

THE LITTLE DOG, (*lowering her eyes*)

Do you mean . . . really?

TOBY-DOG

Of course I do!

THE LITTLE DOG

So soon!

TOBY-DOG

We've already wasted a great deal of time.

THE LITTLE DOG

But . . . we've been chatting. I've enjoyed it very much . . . and I fail to understand why the society of young dogs like you, is forbidden me . . .

TOBY-DOG

Allow me to make love to you.

THE LITTLE DOG

What's that?

TOBY-DOG

I'll show you. First I hold myself very erect, stiffen my legs, walk 'round you, barking low and melodiously. My tail wriggles, my ears . . .

THE LITTLE DOG

Don't come near me. I feel quite upset. (*Escaping.*) Aïe! You unmannerly fellow!

KIKI-THE-DEMURE, (*standing up*)

These preludes are indeed a sad parody on our wild love-making . . . (*aloud, very angry*) I should think—

THE LITTLE DOG *looks to see where the dreadful voice is coming from, and espies a strange striped monster with eyes afire, and eyebrows and whiskers bristling ferociously. She dashes towards the door crying,*

Help, help! There's a tiger on the piano! . . .

And falls into the arms of her mistress, who has come upon the scene and proceeds to console her with great volubility; Fifi! my Zezette! My darling! there, there, goo, goo, goo, goo, you poor helpless little doggie! What did they do to her? Ooooo!—Ooo! Was it the naughty bow-bow? etc., etc., etc.

CPSIA information can be obtained
at www.ICGtesting.com
Printed in the USA
LVHW080953210920
666643LV00011B/81